Co zrobić z bobasem
BUU HUU HUU?

What Shall We Do With The **BOO HOO BABY?**

by Cressida Cowell

Illustrated by Ingrid Godon

Mantra Lingua

Bobas mówi:

The baby said,

For perplexed parents everywhere - C.C.

Falkirk Council	
Askews & Holts	2015
JF JF	£8.50

First Published in 2000 by Macmillan Children's Books, London
First dual language edition published in 2002 by Mantra Lingua
This edition published 2012

Mantra Lingua Ltd
Global House, 303 Ballards Lane, London N12 8NP
www.mantralingua.com

"Buu huu huu!"

"Boo-hoo-hoo!"

Kaczka mówi:
"Kwak?"

"Quack?"
said the duck.

Co zrobić z bobasem
buu huu huu?

What shall we do with
the boo-hoo baby?

"Nakarmić go," - mówi pies.

"Feed him," said the dog.

Więc nakarmili bobasa.

So they fed the baby

"Miau!"
- mówi kot.

"Miaow!"
said the cat.

"Hau!"
- mówi pies.

"Bow-wow!"
said the dog.

"Kwak!"
- mówi kaczka.

"Quack!"
said the duck.

"Muu!"
- mówi krowa,

"Moo!"
said the cow,

a...

and...

Bobas mówi:
"Buu huu huu!"

"Boo-hoo-hoo!"
said the baby.

Co zrobić z bobasem
buu huu huu?
"Wykąpać go,"
- mówi kot.

What shall we do with
the boo-hoo baby?
"Bath him,"
said the cat.

Więc wykąpali bobasa.

So they bathed the baby.

"Kwak!"
- mówi kaczka

"Hau!"
- mówi pies.

"Quack!"
said the duck.

"Miau!"
- mówi kot.

"Bow-wow!"
said the dog.

"Miaow!"
said the cat.

"Muu!"
- mówi krowa,

"Moo!"
said the cow,

a...

and...

Bobas mówi:
"Buu huu huu!"

"Boo-hoo-hoo!"
said the baby.

Co zrobić z bobasem
buu huu huu?
"Bawić się z nim,"
- mówi krowa.

What shall we do with
the boo-hoo baby?
"Play with him,"
said the cow.

Więc bawili się z bobasem.

So they played with the baby.

"Kwak!"
- mówi kaczka

"Hau!"
- mówi pies.

"Miau!"
- mówi kot.

"Quack!"
said the duck.

"Bow-wow!"
said the dog.

"Miaow!"
said the cat.

"Muu!"
- mówi krowa,

"Moo!"
said the cow,

a...

and...

Bobas mówi:
"Buu huu huu!"

"Boo-hoo-hoo!"
said the baby.

Co zrobić z bobasem
buu huu huu?
"Położyć go do łóżeczka,"
- mówi kaczka.

What shall we do with
the boo-hoo baby?
"Put him to bed,"
said the duck.

So they put him to bed.

"Miau!"
- mówi kot.

"Miaow!"
said the cat.

Więc położyli go do łóżeczka.

"Hau!"
- mówi pies.

"Kwak!"
- mówi kaczka.

"Muu!"
- mówi krowa,

"Bow-wow!"
said the dog.

"Quack!"
said the duck.

"Moo!"
said the cow,

a...

and...

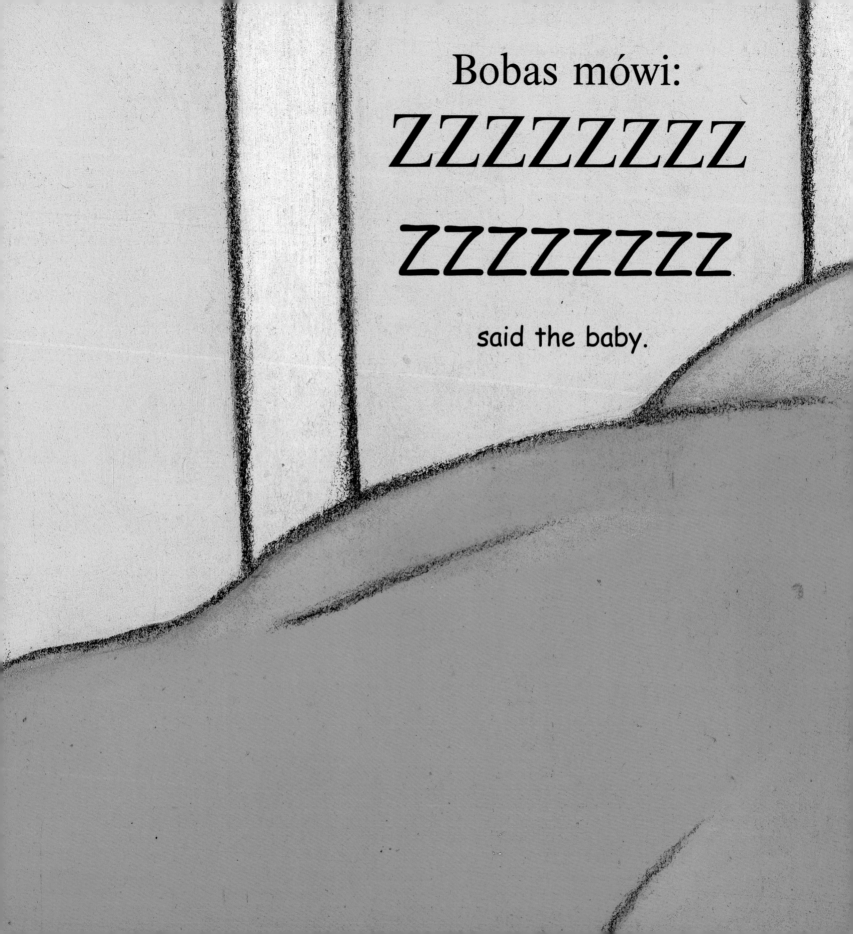

Bobas mówi:

ZZZZZZZZ

ZZZZZZZZ

said the baby.

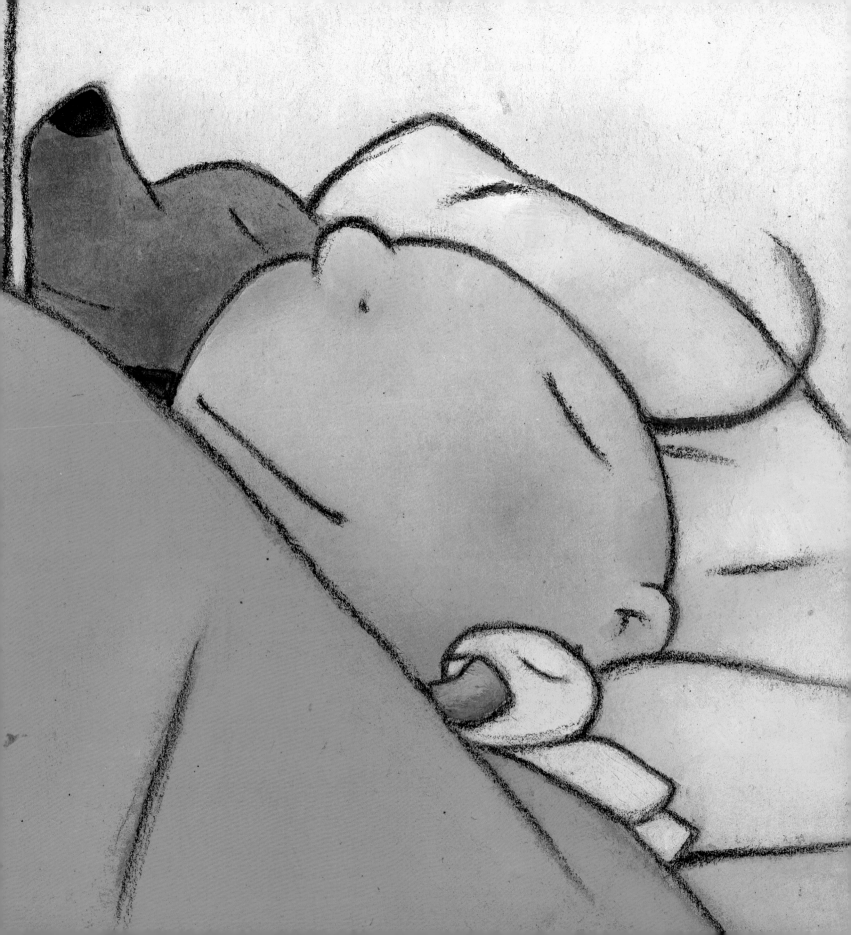